DEDICATION

This book is dedicated to our awesome grandbabies; Korey Jr, Raylen, Kendrick Jr, Quinn, Julian, Jordan, Denise and Kolin, and our wonderful children Kendrick, Korey, Brooke, and Mikaela.

Thanks to my wonderful husband, Michael, for always supporting and pushing me to follow my dreams and encouraging me to use the gifts God has given me. I love you!

Never in my wildest imagination did I consider writing a children's book, but when I began to think about our precious grandbabies. I thought about my love for God and how could I express my love for God to them. How would they understand on such a small level?

The Lord began to impress on my heart...you do it! Do what? You write the book. To my amazement, I was excited and delighted to give our grandbabies such a gift from God. It's my prayer for you that your babies, grandbabies, great grands, nieces, nephews, godchildren & cousins will have an opportunity to experience this book filled with blessings!

I pray for God's word to stick in their hearts and grow as seeds causing them to become great men & women of God! I'm so grateful to the Lord for impressing upon my heart and inspiring me to write this special little book of inspiration for little people.

D1568012

NANA'S INSPIRATION FOR LITTLE PEOPLE

EVERYDAY REMINDERS OF GOD'S WORD

Kim Y. Lyons

Graphic Designer: Lisa Banks

Published by: Anointed Words Publishing Company awpubco@gmail.com

ISBN: 9798430795337

Printed in the United States of America ICB INTERNATIONAL CHILDRENS VERSION.

STAY HAPPY

Korey likes to play with Dinosaurs! It makes him smile. Are you wearing a smile today? God can help you stay happy. He knows what makes you happy and what makes you sad.

Proverbs 15:13 ICB

Happiness makes a person smile.
But sadness breaks a person's spirit.

Prayer

Help me, God, to smile and be happy!

PRACTICE

Raylen, likes to learn new things. She's trying to learn how to ride her new pink bike. God created us to learn new things and grow. He promises to help us if we try. You can learn to do many things if you practice.

Philippians 4:13 ICB

I can do all things through Christ because he gives me strength.

Prayer

Lord help me to practice on the things I don't do well and give me strength to work on it.

WHEN I GROW UP

Kendrick wants to be a doctor when he grows up. We may want to be many things in life, a fireman, teacher, preacher. Whatever you decide you want to be, if you will pray and ask God to help you, He will help you know what He wants you to be.

Proverbs 3:5-6 ICB

Trust the Lord with all your heart. Don't depend on your own understanding. Remember the Lord in everything you do, and he will give you success.

Prayer

God lead and guide my steps every day. Bless me to be what you have created me to be.

LOVE

Quinn loves his dog, Zeus. He loves his toys, and he loves his family. Who do you love? Do you love your parents? Do you love your Nana and Pawpaw? Love is a wonderful gift God has given us. We are able to love others because of God's love.

I John 4:19 ICB

We love because God first loved us.

Prayer

God thank you for the gift of love and thank you for loving me and my family.

LET'S HELP

Julian likes helping his parents clean the house & yard. How do you help at home? Everyone needs to be a helper when there is work to be done. God likes helpers, but he wants us to do it to please him and to make him happy.

So, the next time you see a need to help, help and tell God this is for you! God is happy when people help each other and be kind to one another.

Colossians 3:17 ICB

Everything you say and everything you do should all be done for Jesus your Lord. And in all you do, give thanks to God the Father through Jesus.

Prayer

Lord, help me to do my part & help others.

FOLLOW GOD

Jordan has new gym shoes. His is so happy to go outside and play. Maybe his feet will take him to the park or maybe down the street to a friend's house.

The Bible tells us to walk with God. We can walk with him each and every day. When you obey God and do what is right, you are following & walking with Him.

Psalm 119:133 ICB

Guide my steps as you promised
Don't let any sin control me

Prayer

Dear God, bless me to walk with you every day!

BEDTIME

Denise is ready to go to bed with her big stuffed doll baby. She feels safe when she has it. Do you feel safe in your bed at night? God is always awake & he watches over us. He doesn't get tired like we do and fall asleep.

Psalms 91:11 ICB

**He has put his angels in charge of you.
They will watch over you wherever you go.**

Prayer

Lord, thank you for watching over me and my family while we sleep.

DON'T WORRY

Oh no, Raylen lost her ring. She's worried that her parents will be disappointed with her. But God tells us in the bible that we do not need to worry about anything. God wants us to pray instead of worrying. When we tell God about our concerns, He hears us, and he helps us.

Philippians 4:6 ICB

Do not worry about anything. But pray and ask God for everything you need. And when you pray, always give thanks.

Prayer

Dear God, help me not to worry and to trust you.

10

MAD

Jordan is mad, he is having a temper tantrum because he's disappointed about losing his toy car. Do you ever get mad? If you ever get mad or disappointed, you can ask God to help you be happy again.

Ephesians. 4:26 ICB

When you are angry, do not sin. And do not go on being angry all day.

Prayer

God when I get mad, help me to be happy again.

NOT AFRAID

Julian is getting ready to go to his first swim lesson. He is a little nervous and a little afraid? Have you ever been afraid? Afraid of a dog? Afraid of the dark? What are you afraid of? Do you feel safe when someone you love is close by? The Bible tells us that God is always near us. We can always pray and ask God to protect us, and He will.

II Timothy 1:7 ICB

God did not give us a spirit that makes us afraid. He gave us a spirit of power and love and self-control.

Prayer

God, help me not to be afraid. Help me to walk in faith and trust you!

GIVING

Korey is giving Christmas presents to his Nana & Paw paw. It's fun to open Christmas presents and find out what is inside, but it can also be fun to give a present to someone else.

When you give someone a gift, it makes the person feel happy and that should make you feel happy and special too!

Acts 20:35 ICB

I showed you in all things that you should work as I did and help the weak. I taught you to remember the words of Jesus. He said, 'It is more blessed to give than to receive.

Prayer

Lord, bless me to be a giver.

FEAR

Kendrick's parents turned off the lights for him to go to bed. He heard a noise and became afraid. It was only the dog in his room who wouldn't hurt him. Do you ever feel afraid? Everyone feels afraid now and then. When you are afraid, pray and ask God to protect you and he will.

Psalm 56:3 ICB

When I am afraid, I will trust you.

Prayer

God, help me not to be afraid. Teach me to trust in your power and love for me.

THANKFUL

Denise was so thankful when Nana brought her a strawberry ice cream cone. Do you remember to thank God for all the good things he does for you? God loves to bless us! Remember to give thanks to God for everything He does for you, everyday!

Psalms 118:1 ICB

Thank the Lord because he is good. His love continues forever.

Prayer

Thank you, Lord, for everything you do for me. I love you!

SHARING IS GOOD

Quinn shared his popcorn with the rest of his cousins and saved some for his parents. A generous person gives more than what others expect to get. How can you be generous today? How can you give more?

Luke 6:38 ICB

Give, and you will receive. You will be given much. It will be poured into your hands—more than you can hold. You will be given so much that it will spill into your lap. The way you give to others is the way God will give to you.

Prayer

Lord, help me to share, give and be kind.

PRIZE

Korey and Quinn won medals for playing on the soccer team! Have you ever won a prize or an award for something you've done? Most people like winning prizes. God has prizes for people who love & obey him. God's prizes are called rewards. God will reward us one day when we go to heaven for all the good that we have done.

Ephesians 6:8 ICB

Remember that the Lord will give a reward to everyone, slave or free, for doing good.

Prayer

Lord, help me to do good, obey your word and make you happy!

RULES

Julian & Denise's parents told them not to touch the wall because it was wet from the new paint, but they touched it anyway. They disobeyed their parents. Maybe your parents have rules like, don't touch the stove or don't cross the street before looking both ways. Your parents make rules because they love you and they know what is best for you.

God wants you to obey your parents and when you do, you are obeying God.

Ephesians 6:1 ICB

Children, obey your parents the way the Lord wants. This is the right thing to do.

Prayer

Help me God, to obey my parents.

DOING GOOD

Raylen, Kendrick and Jordan all three of them helped their parents with putting up the groceries and helping clean the house. God likes it when we do good things to help others. What are some things we can do to help others?

Psalm 37:3 ICB

Trust the Lord and do good. Live in the land and enjoy it's safety.

Prayer

Help me to do the things I'm supposed to do and never get tired of doing good.

GOD IS GREAT

Have you ever looked up at the sun? Have you ever watched a beautiful sunset? Have you ever been to the ocean?

God created these awesome things. Even though we can't see God, we can see how great He is by His wonderful creation. God is greater than everything he created.

Psalms 48:1 ICB

The Lord is great; he should be praised in the city of our God, on his holy mountain.

Prayer

God you are Great! I love you!

PRAYER

One of the most important things you can do is pray. Prayer is talking to God. Praying to God is something that boys and girls can do as well as well as grown-ups.

Have you ever prayed for someone who was sad? Have you ever prayed for someone who was sick? When you pray for others, God hears your prayers. Who can you pray for today?

Thessalonians 5:17 ICB

Never stop praying.

Prayer

God, protect me and keep my family and friends safe!

SALVATION

God wants us to live with him in heaven forever. He tells us how we can do it.

John 3:16 ICB

For God loved the world so much that he gave his only Son. God gave his Son so that whoever believes in him may not be lost but have eternal life.

Prayer

Thank you for your son Jesus who you gave for me.

I receive him into my heart as my

Lord and Savior

Amen

NANA'S PRAYER

Lord, bless the reader and hearer of this little book. May their lives be inspired to love and serve you in a great way! May each one fulfill the call and the plan that you have purposed and may a mighty move of your presence be released through their lives.

In Jesus Name

Amen

STAY CONNECTED

Connect with

Kim Lyons Ministries

FACEBOOK/KIM LYONS

INSTAGRAM/@KIMLYONSMINISTRIES

Podcast/Prayer Impact

www.infaithministries.org

Made in the USA
Monee, IL
23 June 2022

98505462R00017